DATING
INTERVENTION

DATING
INTERVENTION

DO'S AND DON'TS TO DODGE DISASTER

TRAVIS BRYANT JR

TouchKC

TouchKC

TouchKC, LLC
Kansas City, MO

Copyright @ 2019 by TRAVIS BRYANT JR
Book & Cover Design by JOSHUA GREEN

For information about special discounts for bulk purchases, please visit touchkc.com

ISBN: 978-1-7335732-0-7

Table of Contents

FOR
anyone looking to cultivate their interpersonal skills

Our relationships are our most important resource.

Preface

So I'm a big "why" guy. I have to know *why* in order to *be motivated* to do. If this resonates, then know you are not alone. I personally believe **why** is more important than **what**. This book was created because I realized that there is a very important element of marriage that is not talked about. If you can imagine marriage as a timeline, usually we focus on the middle (*the middle being the actual marriage*), and we all hope for a pleasant ending. Unfortunately, often times that end is traumatic. Often times that end is divorce. But no one talks about the beginning. **No one talks about how to date.**

Challenge accepted!

With few exceptions, every romantic relationship begins with dating. This is where the timeline starts, and this beginning sets the foundation of everything after. I want to at least spark conversation on how to think about dating, how to approach dating, and how to be safe while dating...all while having fun. Dating is exciting! Dating is awesome! But just like with most things that are incredibly awesome (driving a car for example), if we do not have proper instructions, we can/will hurt ourselves. I would like to offer a solution to this dilemma that we all face from time to time.

The objectives of this book are beautifully simple. By the end of this book, you will be able to:

- Understand the do's and don'ts of dating
- Describe what dating means and what dating does not mean.

As stated earlier, I'm really big on definition. Definition allows clarity, direction, and intention. Consider this: without definition you can't have process; without process you can't have order, and without order there is only chaos. As we journey together, try to be conscious of not just what you are thinking, but *why* you are thinking it.

Introduction

Cognitive dissonance.

It does not matter if I am presenting a seminar on dating or a workshop on how to mentor effectively, I always take time to explain cognitive dissonance. It is a reality that you have to manage, or it will manage you.

Cognitive dissonance occurs when beliefs are contradicted by new information. This conflict activates areas of the brain involved in personal identity and emotional response to threats, real or imagined. This causes the brain's alarms to go off, triggering a person on both a cognitive and emotional level. The person may shut down, or even become violent in response, disregarding any rational evidence that contradicts what they had previously regarded as truth.

Now, I know that's a really technical definition, but cognitive dissonance is something that we all have all experienced at some time or another. If I'm being honest, even though I am very much aware of it, dissonance still catches me off guard from time to time. As an example, have you ever had a friend that was in some ridiculous relationship that has failed several times? This SAME friend claims that they hate the person, yet this SAME friend still ends up in the SAME toxic relationship, hurting themselves over and over again. It always ends badly, but they "love" them. They are willing to give the object of their affection just one more chance—a promise made empty by all the times you've heard it. Finally, being the good friend that you are, you approach them.

You point out the obvious in the friendliest, gentlest, most loving way you know, all in hopes that they might do something different. Surely, they must be unaware. Who would just choose to keep making the same mistake over and over?

Maybe no one that they love and trust has brought this dangerous cycle to their attention.

And what do you get for this effort of love and honesty? Aggravation, if not aggression. You are now the bad guy. They label you without regard to your intentions. They shut down. You have no idea what you did wrong or why they would refuse your help with such venom and anger.

What they experienced was cognitive dissonance. They know everything you are saying is true. They also believe themselves to be smart and intelligent. The truth you are presenting to them tells a story that conflicts with the truth they believe about themselves. A self-defense mechanism kicks in, and you, the messenger, now become the object of their internal struggle. Attacking you is easier than investigating the cause of their inner turmoil. Many friendships have ended over such dilemmas.

Cognitive dissonance occurs when one's truth contradicts reality. This contradiction can be infuriating. "Don't shoot the messenger" is a plea not to mishandle dissonance. I now make that plea. Everyone struggles with dissonance at some point or another. When dissonance knocks on my door, I try to use the irritation as an invitation to look deeper within myself. Something triggered my internal alarm. It would be emotionally irresponsible of me to not at least check on what I believe I am protecting.

Throughout this book, you may experience some dissonance. That's okay. Honestly, the issue is not experiencing dissonance, but ignoring it. If you feel yourself being flabbergasted while reading, make yourself reason through it. Pause. Breathe. Then come back. **Do not let cognitive dissonance rip you away from an opportunity to be healthy.**

DATING DISASTERS:
A LIST OF DON'TS

You're still here? Great!

So, we have not one, not two, not three, but *four* disasters that are the typical destroyers of romantic relationships. One would need to recognize and circumvent these disasters to date effectively.

Dating does not have to be destructive. Healthy relationship building should be a pleasant experience even if things do not go beyond being platonic. And of course, you want a pleasant, healthy experience; otherwise, you wouldn't have picked up this book!

Here are the four disasters to avoid:

1. Lack of intentionality
2. Being in love with being in love
3. Interviewing versus auditioning
4. Putting the cart before the horse

The principles that you are about to learn in this book do not promise to help you "find true love." However, this book does give the proper insight on how to value your time and get the most from the dating experience.

Often what we think is the problem is not really the problem. Instead, how we think about the problem is the actual problem.

Read on if you are interested in addressing and solving the dating crisis in your life. It will be uncomfortable at times. If you are looking for a quick fix...this is not the book for you. However, if you are really looking to make some significant differences in how you approach dating, I applaud you.   Not only are you showing awareness by seeing that there is a problem, but you are also taking steps to do something about it.   I am honored to be a part of your process.

CHAPTER 1

LACK OF INTENTIONALITY

"We sail within a vast sphere, ever drifting in uncertainty, driven from end to end.

Blaise Pascal

LACK OF
INTENTIONALITY

So here's the thing—dating is about you. You are valuable. Your time is valuable. For any of the concepts of this book to make sense, you have to embrace this reality. You are valuable everywhere you go. Any place you enter instantly becomes different because you are there.

You are valuable.

Don't let anyone tell you differently. The greatest part about dating effectively is understanding that dating is about you. And when you believe something is valuable, you are very intentional with how you handle it and who you let handle it. To put yourself in a physical situation without really thinking is dangerous. But when you put yourself in an emotional situation without thinking; it can be traumatic.

Be aware of your emotional state. We have seen what happens when matters of the heart are handled carelessly. Devastation and heartbreak, resentment and shame; these negative experiences are often the result of being careless. They don't have to be included in the dating experience. These are things you can avoid, but when you are not intentional, that means you are moving to someone else's agenda.

I'll give an example. Have you ever gone to the grocery store without a plan? You had just money and your hunger. You go to the store because you are hungry and hope for the best. Walmart is counting on you, your hunger pangs, and your wallet. A most dangerous combination.

If you're anything like me, now you're at the cash register with a whole bunch of stuff that you really don't need, challenging your budget in ways that are completely unnecessary. The cashier rings you up. Now you have to choose between praying that your debit swipe doesn't betray you or require you to make that long walk of shame, replacing items you didn't need in the first place. And think, this is just grocery shopping. It is even more dangerous when we tie ourselves emotionally to people without being intentional.

Dating while being lonely and distraught has some parallels to grocery shopping while hungry; you can end up paying for what you never should have purchased in the first place. Remember, you are valuable. If you have forgotten that, or if you find yourself wondering if it is true...then don't date. You are a starving person at Walmart. Time is the currency, every isle an opportunity to spend. An hour later, you are still wandering the isles, looking for fulfillment. In dating, you can waste a lot of time and resources simply because you were unsure of what you were looking for in the first place and you allowed your emotional state to influence your decision making. This is very dangerous indeed.

Know Your Agenda.

There was something I read recently about the psychology behind grocery store aesthetics. Placement, colors, even the music, are all purposely placed with the intention for the consumer to . . .well . . . *consume*.

You don't need any ice cream; you probably have ice cream at home, but why not? You may believe that you wanted ice cream, but in truth, some companies actually hire a psychologist to help them set you up. If you go there without intention, then you are following their agenda. Similarly, if you are dating without intention, then you are following the other person's agenda.

You are more valuable than that—drifting without purpose. You don't know where you'll land. As I will say again and again throughout this book, your time, resources, and effort are too valuable for just "*hoping for the best.*"

Here is a phrase to remember (especially around the holidays): **Don't let loneliness make a fool out of you.**

Relationships are too important to our well-being. Don't just "drift" into them. Be selective, be intentional, have a plan. If you are dating to just have fun, that's okay. But be upfront about it. Communicate your intentions. Things may change . . . and that's okay, too. But be aware, be vocal, be honest. I'm not just talking about being honest with yourself, but also with others. So much emotional static occurs because of lack of transparency with self and others.

Delay intimacy.
The word of the day is situationship (*Webster eat your heart out!*). A situationship occurs when the

content of the relationship doesn't match the label given. For example, you are "friends" (label) but are also sexually involved and living together (content). Situationships should be avoided. Here are some signs that you know you are in a situationship:

- **"What are we?"** If you have to ask . . . then you know exactly where you are. A situationship.

- **"We're just talking."** For my readers not of the urban core, this is an urban code for "I don't really know what is happening, but I'm developing feelings and hoping that the other person feels the same, based on very thin evidence."

- **"Friends with benefits."** This is a title that says nothing at all. All friendships should be beneficial. It sounds like a grown up thing, only to be handled by the sexually mature. But do you think you can have one side of sex (climaxes, relief, affection) and not the other (attachment, bonding, desire?) Don't fool yourself. "Friends with benefits" is a situation that comes with a timer. It's a game of hot potatoes, and who ever cares first loses. You are too "mature" for that.

- **"Your relationship has to be a secret."** Why are you ashamed? Sure, I understand how people can be nosey and make things dramatic. But there is a difference from keeping something secret and keeping something private. More times than not, you are hiding from your friends and family because you know that what you are doing is foolish, and don't want your honest friend to tell you about yourself.

If any of these points define a relationship you are in—congrats! You are in a situationship! Stop telling people "it's complicated." At least be honest with yourself and the person you are dealing with. It's one thing to take a fruitless risk.

It's another to be in denial about it.

Here is a truth, even for the most introverted individuals—you want to connect. I want to connect. Everyone wants to connect! So, now you are connecting haphazardly to a person in a desperate attempt to deal with your own loneliness, to deal with the hunger that you have. "A hungry man walks into a grocery store" ... if you remember that analogy from earlier, you can see that making decisions while in a desperate state of mind or condition can be dangerous.

Before you have cognitively assessed what you are signing up for, now, intimacy has been created. Intimacy is a glue that gives the greatest high. This is why the "friend" who was in that bad relationship can't get out of it. They are addicted to the intimacy and the connection it provides.

I used to play this game with magnets when I was younger (and so did you). I would take two magnets and see how close I could get them without touching. It would take so much control, and I could not maintain it indefinitely. Unless I completely and intentionally placed them down a safe distance apart, they always snapped together, sometimes startling me. Human beings are very similar in regards to affection and attraction. There is such a deep need for validation, that it doesn't take much for us to be pulled in. **Attraction, time, and opportunity are the main ingredients to form intimacy.**

In your mind, you were going to regulate how close your *magnets* would be. "*Oh, you know, but we aren't going to let it get that that far.*" But that's not a plan. That's bravado. Now you're in another situationship; your best friends are pleading with you to escape. Now you are mad at them, as intimacy, which is beautiful in the right context, now creates chains that are hard to escape. Dating has become something else. The content of your relationship and your label aren't matching.

Honestly? Dating is just really getting to know a person intentionally. That's it. Take a business date. Getting to know another for a specific reason, whether it is a possible partnership or creating a marketing strategy, it's just getting to know a person. When intimacy gets involved, something changes. Please hear me out. Follow the logic. Think about your closest platonic relationship. Was physical intimacy necessary to get to know them? Of course, not. In fact, when a person is trying to rush intimacy, that should be treated as a red flag. It is an attempt to rush an emotional connection before addressing things cognitively. If you haven't caught it yet, **dating should be a cognitive process.**

When it is purely an emotional one, when intimacy is out of context, you'll find yourself in these dangerous situations. The bruises and scars might happen even when you are cognitive. But the horror stories usually happen due to failed expectations that were made only in the context of emotional fulfillment.

Don't do that.

Ladies, when he approaches you, all handsome and educated and full of compliments and expensive cologne, feel free to be flattered. There is nothing wrong with that. If he finds you attractive, please, investigate that possible blessing. But your own desperate desire to belong to someone will cause you to add other expectations prematurely. No, he is not the one. No, he is not proposing tomorrow. It's a compliment. Yes, you are beautiful—and so are dogs, cats, and mice. **Emotional stimulation is not a sign of commitment, but of observation.** That's it.

Make him actually clarify his intentions, and then *hold him to that.* Gentlemen, don't let her trap you with a commitment when you are just dating. Marriage is a commitment of a lifetime, not a gift for her "being there for you." Define where you are, what you are, and be clear of your intentions. If you are only getting to know each other, that is fine. If you are trying to do more than that, that is fine, too. Be clear, be concise, and be wise. Remember: While you were playing with action figures, she was playing with baby dolls, pretending that the Baby Alive was her baby. She has been groomed to want a family. You have to address the issue directly and honestly.

CHAPTER 2

BEING IN LOVE WITH BEING IN LOVE

> One of the definitions of sanity is the ability to tell real from unreal. Soon we'll need a new definition.

Alvin Toffler

BEING IN LOVE WITH BEING IN LOVE

"Feeling" voids.

You like that play on words? I know. Me too! This is actually one of my favorite things to talk about. It is also a most disastrous phenomenon when dating. "Being in love with being in love" is often disguised with self-appointed titles such as *hopeless romantic*, *a bleeding heart*, etc. Of course, I'm not here to judge. It actually makes sense why being "in love" seems to be such an aspired goal. If you can relate to this...it's not your fault. We were all set up to fail, even before we realized what we were failing at.

Ever since we were children, the notion of being attracted to the idea of a relationship *rather than the actual person* was forced upon us.

Relationship equals happiness, and who doesn't want to be happy? Now, if you could only find a bad boy with a good heart like Aladdin, or find a woman who is cultured, sophisticated, humble, and as beautiful as Jasmine, then you can ride off into the sunset. The idea that "true love" is out there—somewhere—just waiting for someone with a heart of gold (*cough* YOU *cough cough*) to find it is a dangerous fantasy.

This idea that being in a relationship somehow solves character issues or the idea that "true love" will somehow make everything better is a foolish notion that kills relationships before they even start. **It creates the idea that chemistry is the relationship, not a byproduct of a healthy one.**

That. Doesn't. Work. In. Real. Life.

Unfortunately, this isn't a Disney movie. In Disney, whole relationships grow, build, then climax before your very eyes. Aladdin is one of my favorite movies. Sure, he was a thief and a liar, but he could sing, dance, all the while dodging the police. And still had a heart of gold. Then, the princess came and changed his life. Sure, they had some problems, but they were able to resolve their issues within an hour and a half.

No one is asking about Aladdin and Jasmine's relationship after twenty years of marriage. That's not romantic. That's not hot. That's not sexy. That "in love" feeling—that energy—we want to rewind that over and over again. But it is dangerous. Dangerous, because we love to love the emotional high instead of the person. It's dramatic. It makes us feel alive. But when you lack intentionality and you have intimacy out of context, you are setting yourself up for fantasy. You'll forget you are dealing with a real life person.

Here's a secret. You don't need anyone else to feel complete because no one else CAN complete you. People can only complement what you're already trying to do, or aid you in evolving who you already are.

Imitations of life.

When we talk about "being in love with being in love," we are just imitating what we believe is making other people happy. Social media encourages that illusion. Consider this scenario: You are at home with Netflix and leftover pizza. You have been looking forward to this all day, just some time to relax. You click on one of your many open tabs and see all these pictures of people traveling. They seem so happy. So happy in fact, that actual sentences take too long to express their happiness . . . #loveforlife #ilovemyboo #lovemesomeUS!

It looks appealing. It makes you look at your own situation and forget how great your situation is. You forget the fact that you are out here handling your business. You forget the fact that you earned your degree and that you are working hard; or even without a degree, you are out here making things happen. You forget all of that because your friend on Facebook seems to be in this wonderful, fulfilling relationship. Their snapshots of happiness have made your previous contentment pale and unrewarding. They look so beautiful. You are in your PJ's and doo-rag, with Dorito dust on your fingers. You suddenly don't feel worth much, and are now questioning your very existence.

Stop that. It's a trap. Normal moments never compare to snapshots. This is only appealing because it seems that your Facebook friend has found their Aladdin/Jasmine, and all they are missing is the magic carpet. What you don't see is the struggle, the pain, the compromises...until suddenly, there are no more pictures. No more hashtags. They had problems you never knew about, and no magical lamp could fix it. Don't let the imitations of life fool you into believing your life isn't awesome, because it is! And if it's not awesome, then why are you looking to date anyway? Take care of you.

CHAPTER 3

INTERVIEWING VERSUS AUDITIONING

> " I have a hard time with interviews, because
> I'd rather hear about the interviewer.
>
> **Maria Bamford**

INTERVIEWING VERSUS AUDITIONING

BF/GF DANGER!

Before we get deep into this, there is something I have to say. Do you remember how we talked about dissonance earlier and I told you there might be a time when you need to pause?

That time is now.

The boyfriend/girlfriend relationship model is a useless and very risky way to build an interpersonal foundation, if marriage is the goal. Commonly, being a boyfriend or girlfriend is treated like a marriage, with all the bonding and expectation that comes with having a spouse, without an actual commitment being made. In truth, you are either too old for a boyfriend/girlfriend or you are too young for a boyfriend/girlfriend.

You are too young because you do not understand what it means to be bonded with another human being. You are too old because you are too busy being effective and impactful to ACT like you're in a marital situation. And if you are not being impactful and trying to figure out your goals and dreams, then what are you going to do with a boyfriend or girlfriend?

Here is another secret. And please gentlemen, don't be angry with me. A man who is growing in his path will know within six months whether he wants to get married or not. Girlfriend is just a pen holder, *"I'm not ready, but I don't want you to go anywhere."* So, now you have been with this girl for four years; that's a whole college degree! All you have to show for it is hashtags and pictures.

You are valuable.

If you are looking towards marriage, towards a lasting commitment, the boyfriend/girlfriend relationship model doesn't not give a very realistic perspective of what married life would look like. There is this idea that if he is a good boyfriend, then he will make a good husband. Or, if she is a good girlfriend, then she will make a good wife. Have you ever heard married couples complain that their spouse seems like a stranger in the marriage? It is my belief that this is mainly due to them believing that "test driving" the relationship would prepare for "spousal-ship" (*and yes, I just made that word up, but I like it, so it stays*). That is like saying that test driving a car will prepare you to be a truck driver. It is true that they are both vehicles of transport, but they require very different skill sets to operate, mainly due to size, and the type of loads they are meant to carry. This is not even talking about the different laws and rules that now apply to operating a big rig versus a little Corolla. Isn't it interesting how we assume a truck driver can drive a Buick, but we do not assume just because a person can drive a jeep, they are prepared to drive a semi?

In case you are still scratching your head, a boyfriend/girlfriend relationship model is the car. It might be a Pinto, might be a Mustang, but a car nonetheless. No matter how long you are driving in the car with that special someone, it does not mean they are ready to drive a semi with you.

That is why he will tell you he is not ready to be your husband, but more than willing to be your boyfriend. Even he is acknowledging that there is a difference. I have been a boyfriend before. My wife is my best friend. This was true before she became my girlfriend; this was true even after we broke up. The title really just added a burden to our relationship. But I wanted the label out of fear. Fear is not a good pillar to build a relationship on.

In truth, it really, really does not take that long to get to know another adult. Think about all the people you are closest to. Did you have to be intimate with them to get to know them that well? Did you have to live with them for years? Did they have to become your "boo-thang" for you to know and understand them?

Absolutely not! That's what makes dating so great! It is safely getting to know a person, especially for adults who have to be intentional due to their busy schedules. We are who we are because that is who we have been. But don't take my word for it. Find your boyfriend or girlfriend, even an ex that you still have a friendship with and read this chapter together. And after your discussion, make sure they buy a copy of their own. Authors have to eat, too!

Accountability is something most of us do not like, but having an open dialogue with the person you care about will help you both put things in proper perspective. Some of the ideas expressed in this chapter will help you both not only decide what type of transport you are using as you journey on this road called life, but may also make sure your GPS is calibrated. Many are traveling together, believing they are on the same page, but have COMPLETELY different destinations in mind.

Interviewing and auditioning.

So what does boyfriend/girlfriend and other situationships have to do with interviewing vs. auditioning? I'll explain. Interviewing should happen during the dating process. Background checks, health history, strengths, work history, weaknesses, etc—this all happens during the dating process. No commitments are made, no emotional ties hardened. It is an exciting adventure that should only be costing you time.

As things progress to courtship, then the auditioning begins. Making serious plans for the future, deepening the emotional bonding (still without sexual reinforcement), plans of marriage this is a very short, but important element in culture building for marriage. But a boyfriend or girlfriend? It fits in neither dating nor courtship, and is more of a hindrance than a help.

Cultivating a relationship is a cognitive process. Love is a cognitive process. Does it stimulate and even satisfy us emotionally? Of course! But using only your heart to guide you will create a bonding process you are possibly not ready for.

If you are just dating, make sure that you're interviewing. Have your resume on hand. Your resume is not on a sheet of paper (*though that isn't a bad idea*), but it is the work you have put into carving out your skills and shaping your dreams; it is the work you put in to enhance your character. This is the work you want to show. And if he or she wants to be a part of your future, then they need to have a resume that shows that they have been working as hard as you are. Show me a resume. You don't have to have a girlfriend or boyfriend for that to happen. You don't have to be sexually active for that to happen. You are valuable as is your time. Act accordingly.

CHAPTER 4

PUTTING THE CART BEFORE THE HORSE

> What is common sense isn't common practice.

Stephen Covey

PUTTING THE CART BEFORE THE HORSE

Marriage should not be the goal . . . a healthy marriage should be.

A young lady I was counseling was very excited about getting married. She had her wedding colors picked out. She knew the type of dress she wanted. She already had decided the guest list, the length of the wedding, and what songs would be on the playlist. The destination was picked and secured, along with the amount of money she was willing to spend. She also knew how many children she was going to have, what their names would be, and the order she would have them in. She was very detailed, and very, VERY serious. And all this would be great, or at least typical, if she hadn't forgotten one critical detail. She forgot an *actual* husband. She created a whole plan which required another person . . . without the other person. But this is common when people think about relationships. It is a very selfish perspective that we are all guilty of. Because our dreams, our fantasies, only involve us. This is not good for relationships. It's not good for you.

So what are some other examples of putting the cart before the horse? A very popular one is when he has gone out with you twice, and he is already creating a future for you both. Another is having children before a relationship has proven stable enough to not crumble under the weight of starting a family.

I am sure that you can name a few more. Regardless of the scenario, it often includes interacting deeply with hypothetical situations that have not been logically thought out. The combination of wanting a certain effect and not rationalizing the pieces needed can create an uncomfortable and unnecessary position in general. This is especially true with relationship building.

You can get so deep in your head that you can't see anything or anyone else; all these expectations in your head for a situation that requires two people. You are so excited about reaching a destination, you do not even care who you go with, or if the cart is hitched correctly, or if the horse has been fed—nothing. You want to run through the stages of relationship development, and skip to the happily ever after. A healthy marriage should be the goal ONLY after someone has shown themselves to possibly be a suitable mate. The status of marriage must not be more important than the person you are building it with. To do otherwise is nuts. Crazy. Have you asked yourself if you are a crazy person lately? Of course, you are. So am I. That's why we need these principles to guide us, lest we be the greatest deterrent to our need for relationship fulfillment. It is okay to hang out. But when you put the cart before the horse, you end up flipping the cart over or hurting the horse. Often, it is both.

When we make marriage the goal before we have even taken the time to understand the dating process, three things can happen (*sometimes simultaneously*):

1. You end up running away sane individuals.

2. You put a lot of pressure on yourself that's unnecessary and that leads to complications.

3. You get to the finish line and realize you hate the prize.

So how do we avoid putting the cart before the horse in our rush to find a mate?

Take your time.

If marriage is a lifetime, why are you rushing? Religion, children, marriage. These are the three most important decisions you will ever make. Rushing to commit to any of them is a fool's errand.

Think.

This sounds so simple. But when the heart gets involved too deeply, it cares less about the horse, the cart, or the road that will be travelled. It only cares about the moment occurring and how to get what it wants or to protect itself from what it doesn't. What I have seen over and over again is that people think about what they want, but not about what it would take to get it. That is not the heart's job. That's the brain's job. Think.

Separate fact from fantasy.

More often still, people do not want whatever thing they are obsessing over. They want the effect that they believe it would give them. But because they didn't think, now they are frustrated and feel betrayed. I've worked with women that want a husband but don't necessarily want to be a wife or even know what that means. I've worked with men that wanted a wife but have no idea what husbandship entails.

They just wanted the things they believed that a marriage would give them, whether that be status, prestige, or an easy life. However, you don't purchase candy without checking the price tag first. Ground yourself in reality. Ask the hard questions. Better now than later.

DATING DISASTERS:
A LIST OF DO'S

We've spent a lot of time thus far making sure that we are thinking about dating in the right way. The dating process can be beautiful, but if done incorrectly, it can be very hazardous. With this newfound knowledge, here are some things to do if you come across a person where there is some type of attraction or mutual interest.

The four P's of practical dating are:

- **Prepare** Yourself.
- **Position** Yourself.
- **Practice** Paranoia.
- **Pamper** Yourself.

Remember, you are made up of all this valuable

data, talent, and experience. Read further to learn how to protect your value without gambling with your heart.

CHAPTER 5

PREPARE YOURSELF

> By failing to prepare, you're preparing to fail.

Benjamin Franklin

PREPARE YOURSELF

Gauge your emotional state.

My oldest daughter is 15 years old, and her current schedule is very demanding. In addition to an accelerated high school program, she is also taking college courses. But in all of her teenage wisdom, and through much trial and error and prayers, she has come to realize something very profound, yet also very simple: Preparation is vitally important to a plan succeeding. A few semesters of college can teach some hard lessons about failure to prepare.

Some of you are coming from some really rough situations. You didn't have this book as a guide, and the world left you beaten and bruised. But you are a warrior and you are pressing on anyway.

I commend you. Before going back out, however, deal with your trauma first. A relationship gone bad is one of the worst things to endure. You need to be honest about your emotional state and your ability to risk disappointment. Everything costs. Even dating healthily comes with a price—the risk of disappointment, the risk of hurt, all within acceptable reason. But when a person is already raw, even the slightest of agitations can burn and blister.

If you are in a situationship, let it go. If you have a boyfriend or girlfriend who after reading this book you can see is a dead end, let it go. You have people in your life that have harmed you. Address them. Forgive them. Let it go. If you need to seek therapy, then do that. If you need to talk to a friend, do that. If you need to be alone, do that.

But you will only know what you need when you're honest about your emotions. Don't let your feelings make a fool of you. If you know you're in a situation where your loneliness is so great that you will attach to anything, be honest. Don't put the cart in front of the horse by entertaining the possibility of companionship and you haven't found the courage to at least confront yourself.

Your first priority is you.

People depend on you, so you owe it to them to take care of yourself. When I work with parents, they have the hardest time understanding this concept. *"No, my kids are the most important."* There is no glory in martyrdom.

Consider this: If you have ever flown before, shortly after taking your seat, a flight attendant directs your attention to the front. Usually this is the part we all tune out. Just a bunch of safety tips and instruction in case something goes wrong at 40,000 feet. Nothing to give your undivided attention to. Candy Crush high scores won't beat themselves.

Anyway, one of the safety details they really emphasize is what to do in the case of an oxygen shortage or if the cabin loses pressure. They show how an oxygen mask will drop from above. In a very impressive theatrical demonstration, they give very precise instructions when using the mask. One instruction in particular seems most absurd. The flight attendant tells you to first secure your mask before assisting another person. It may seem counterintuitive, but the logic is, again, simple: Help yourself so you will be in a position to help someone else. You have to make sure you are okay, because if you don't, both you and the other person can end up suffocating. Before dating, you need to make sure you are okay first. You are going to be a blessing to someone. They can wait for your greatness to heal.

Another part of preparation is making sure you know why you are dating. Be honest with your intentions and stick to them. The body does not listen to reason. You know your pattern and what type of environments triggers for you. If you are not sure, go back to the section titled *Lack of Intentionality.* Know your agenda. Read through that chapter a hundred times if you have too. But this is important to understand before you go out and present yourself to someone.

Be safe.

The grim truth is that the world is a crazy place. Always meet in public places first. Let a few close friends know where you are going. Develop a text code to alert them if you are in danger. Take a picture of you and your date, and send it to the friend you trust. Let your date know what you are doing and why. If they can't understand that, consider it a red flag and leave. You are dating smart now. You want to engage someone who sees that as a sign of intelligence, not insecurity. And yes, guys, these safety tips are for you, also.

Take heed.

CHAPTER 6

POSITION YOURSELF

> The two most important requirements for major success are, first, being in the right place at the right time, and second, doing something about it.

Ray Kroc

POSITION YOURSELF

Self-development.

A question that people seem to love to ask is: "*How do I attract people?*" This is a very fair question. I'm going to tell you something my father told me. He said, "*Son, work on you, and they will come.*" Very rarely were truer words ever spoken. This was one of the best pieces of advice my father ever gave me about dating, and it has stood the test of time. Developing yourself and unlocking your potential is one of the most attractive things you can do for yourself. The world has taken a great interest in physical enhancements. It seems that plastic and silicon are major parts of the new wave. I wish that it would drown. But to each their own. The type of enhancements I'm speaking of can be broken into three parts: Physical, Intellectual, and Spiritual.

Physical.

This has to do with taking care of your body. A person who doesn't look like they can care for themselves does not appear as if they can take care of others. Find a style that fits you. Buy clothes that fit you. Emphasize healthy eating habits. Hit the gym. Intentionality with self sends out a signal to others. This is not about being thin, (*skinny does not mean healthy*) but maximizing the shape you are in. That type of effort sends out a signal. *"This is what my attention looks like. Imagine if I paid attention to you?"* To avoid vanity, make sure you are paying attention to the other two points that follow.

Intellectual.

To begin, school is not really a good measure of intelligence. But that is another soapbox for another day. The intelligence I am talking about is the ability to reason, the ability to learn, and the ability to apply. Develop skills. Of course, I am not just saying this for you to attract a person. You really should develop your skills and talents for you. Find your interest. Build, create, and evolve, constantly pushing some aspect of yourself to be better than yesterday. What are your goals and passions?

Here is a quick assignment:

1. List five goals for yourself. Then list what it would take to accomplish those tasks.

2. Make a list of what you are missing (*whether that be skills or resources*) that may be keeping you from your goals. For example, if you want to be a wife, then list what skills are necessary for you to be what you consider a great wife.

3. Pledge to yourself that you are going to invest in yourself to complete those goals.

This requires thinking, planning, and executing. This requires intelligence. People believe that confidence is what attracts people. I disagree. I believe it's competence. Confidence is the by-product of competence. Don't make the mistake in believing that you have to wait on someone to unlock your potential. You can do that all by yourself. Position yourself to be relatable. Position yourself to be datable. Because silicone butt shots only go so far. Grow your mind. Read. Travel. You have no skyline; you have no horizon.

Spiritual.

I am a Christian. I am a strong believer in the Bible and I have no shame about that. My spirituality gives me confidence. Not confidence that comes from some sense of false bravado, but one that comes from having faith in something bigger than myself. I believe in something that helps me understand the inner me, heal the inner me, and find peace with my inner me. I don't impose my beliefs on people. But I will say this: Until you have found healing of your emotional state, until you have made peace with yourself, you will be tempted to ask a person to fill that void.

Unfortunately, no *one* person can. I can offer you Jesus, but then you might slip into some dissonance you have against what you define as religion, and this book has already given you enough to think about. But if you are ever curious, hit me up. I would love to talk to you about my process and about my God.

CHAPTER 7

PRACTICING PARANOIA

> To most people, paranoia carries a negative connotation. I believe it is one of the most valuable attributes a leader can have. It is about self-reflection and having the courage, humility, and discipline to constantly ask uncomfortable questions that can potentially poke holes in your strategy and challenge your conventional thinking.

Dinesh Paliwal

PRACTICING PARANOIA

You are incredible, but the universe doesn't care. There are so many myths when it comes to relationships. But there are a few that make anywhere I'm standing turn into an instant soapbox. I make it a personal mission to confront and debunk certain ideologies that I know to be dangerous.

Here is another secret.

There is this belief that because you are important and valuable and full of self-love, the universe will treat you the way you treat others. That is just not true. Being confident, being kind, being honest, does not ensure … well … anything. When working with parents, I have noticed this tendency for instilling self-confidence in children. This idea that boosting a child's ego somehow translates to self-love and acceptance is a fallacy that creates a poor worth ethic and a sense of entitlement. Stop that.

Telling children that they are kings and queens does not prepare them to be good at it. It makes them feel as if they already are. Now the child grows up with this huge sense of entitlement without any skills to justify it. You can instill competence without lying.

We don't only lie to our children, however, we also lie to ourselves. You are so confident in your will power, that you believe that by just telling yourself something, somehow it will happen. So many self-promises, just to find yourself in another situation which you had promised yourself would "*never happen again*" because you "*deserve better.*" When I speak of paranoia, it is easy to understand why you may assume I am talking about being paranoid of the dangers others may present.

I'm not; I'm talking about you being paranoid of *you*.

Pay attention to patterns.

You can believe what comes out of a man's mouth, or you can believe a man's actions. If you choose the former rather than the latter, please go back to page one. You should trust a person's pattern over their words. This should be the rule when dating one another.

But more importantly, this should be the rule when you evaluate yourself. There is who you think you are, who you wish you were, how other people see you, how you see yourself, and how you wish other people would see you. The only way to have any chance of seeing your true self is by looking through a rear view mirror at your past decisions. The "true you" lies in the decisions you have already made. Embrace that. Respect that. But don't overlook it because you don't like that.

In my experience, when you are able to accept that your past decisions have a huge impact on your present thought process, you are able to effectively plan. But when you are in denial, you are inviting the same disasters to take place over and over again. It is time to break cycles. And, believe me, it is hard.

I have a love affair with chocolate. It's pretty bad. Like, "*steal from your kids and act like it is because you love them*" bad, but I refused to believe I had a problem. I could stop anytime I wanted.

Sound familiar?

Anyway, I am pretty familiar with the importance of health. I know that what I call chocolate is really just chocolate flavored at best. I am aware of how sugar destroys the immune system. I've taught lessons on the subject. Unfortunately, knowledge has never really saved anyone, and I am no exception. When I felt a cold coming on, I knew what I should do. Tumeric, garlic, onion, lemon, with mint. Lots of water, lots of sleep, and absolutely, positively no sugar. Then, I happened to come across a Snickers. I knew I shouldn't. I knew that, if I had to, I could ignore the urge. I told myself that I could be responsible and sensible for my health's sake. It was only a couple of days that I would have to do without. All I had to do was give my body a chance to heal. I could do it.

However, there was nothing in my many years of living to suggest that I would make such a responsible decision. In fact, quite the opposite. Denying my past and speaking positively to my future meant nothing. Therefore, a cold that should have been gone within a few days matured into a full-on immunological attack, to which there was no mercy. There is nothing wrong with hope. But by choosing hope and ignoring your past patterns, you are dooming yourself to failure.

So for your own protection, here are some things to consider when practicing paranoia:

Wisdom is better than strength.
Had I embraced my pattern, I would have known that it would have been better to avoid a showdown with a candy bar than to try to endure it. Did I mention that the Snickers wasn't even mine? Dark times.

Trust your tendencies over your intentions.
This means that if every Netflix and chill intention has turned into regret the next morning...trust that. Even if you believe that this time would be different. It won't be different until you do something different.

Practice trusting yourself with smaller, less detrimental things.
Abstinence is hard. It is even harder when you

attempt to test your resilience in an intimate setting. Sure, you want to prove it to yourself, but try practicing your new found will on something less detrimental . . . like candy bars.

Do not trust recent successes.

Do not assume because you have some success at playing with fire without getting burned that you are now flame proof. Be smart. Be intentional. Do not assume that because you are actually doing a good job with dating properly that you can now let your guard down. Continue to be intentional with your body, time, and space.

Be safe.

It's a crazy world, and people are crazier. Yes, they may seem charming. Yes, they may seem educated. That does not mean that they don't dress up as pigeons when no one is looking; I'm not judging. I'm just saying be careful. Don't be so quick to judge. Take your time.

This does not mean accuse them of things that you have not witnessed, but be comfortable with the idea that you do not know. Enjoy yourself. Getting to know people is awesome! But, proceed with caution.

CHAPTER 8

PAMPER YOURSELF

> Self-care is the non-negotiable. That's the thing that you have to do. And beauty is the thing that can be the benefit of the self-care. Beauty is not the point. Beauty is just a cute side-effect from self-care.

Jonathan Van Ness

PAMPER
YOURSELF

You are a priority. Even among mental health professionals, self-care isn't spoken of enough. There are many reasons for this, but we will only focus on a few.

One reason self-care is neglected is because our expectation revolves around just surviving rather than thriving. You are meant to achieve more than not dying. Surviving (*in most cases*) doesn't require much, so much care doesn't seem to be needed.

Another possible reason why self-care is ignored is because we don't believe that we need to make time for ourselves. We have so many deadlines to meet, so many responsibilities and obligations, that taking time out for ourselves seems selfish, instead of necessary.

Finally, we will address my personal favorite—the glorification of emotional martyrdom. We touched on this a bit earlier. There is an idea that there is bravery in pushing until exhaustion—and not stopping. *"I'll rest when I'm dead"* some rich rapper yelled into his mic. But if you go to his Instagram page, there is a picture of him relaxing on a cruise ship. He knows the importance of self-care. Yes, work hard. But you must take care of the machine that makes all this hard work possible—you.

The only thing all martyrs have in common is that they all die. The casket comes for all. Don't go to your grave with only grit to show for it. Take care of self, and self will take care of you. How does this connect to dating? Because "hating your life" is an easy way to find yourself looking for someone to free you from your own disdain. The bad news is, no one can do that for you.

So feed you. Do something fun. Pick up a new hobby. Go out with friends. Take yourself to the movies. I'm a married man, and I still do that from time to time. In fact, it is needed as much as ever when you are married, but that is for another book. Play basketball. Anything (*safe*) that allows you to temporarily escape the grind you are constantly on. Your body needs your care. Your mind needs your care. Your spirit needs your care.

You are priority. Find a community. Invest in a social life so that when this person does come in, they are not your end all, be all. You are responsible for your actions. Go and just unplug for a while. You've heard the cliché "*date yourself first?*" As much as I am not a fan of clichés, this one rings true. If you are not comfortable in your own space, you will hold others responsible for making you comfortable. That is not their responsibility.

Pamper yourself, fellow dreamer. Don't feel guilty about that. You deserve it. Life is hard enough.

CHAPTER 9

DATING DOES & DOES NOT MEAN

> I have always written only for myself—to clarify things, to clarify things with myself, to understand in an inner way what is actually happening.

Herta Muller

DATING DOES & DOES NOT MEAN

So how should we define dating?

Dating is intentionally getting to know another person by setting aside time for a relationship to develop.

We are adults, and very busy. There is this idea that there aren't any good men/women left. I say that there are . . . they are just in their homes, waiting to be kidnapped by the 'right' person. Go out! Have fun! There are actually awesome people out there!

Dating is an interactive interview.

It is about two great people feeling each other out to see if a merger is beneficial. Dating is just getting to know another person on purpose. That is all. That is it.

Dating does require you to feel comfortable in your own space.
Otherwise, there is a temptation to put the cart before the horse. Progress does not happen that way. Date yourself. Discover your flaws and shortcomings. This does not mean wait until you are perfect. It means wait until you are ready.

Dating does mean you are certain that you are uncertain.
There is a freedom and excitement in this. However, be safe. You have no obligations. Self-paranoia is your best friend. And don't be afraid to ask questions. Be yourself. You are only showing what you have been building all your life. You may not be for everybody, and that's okay. Follow your intuition. If you feel like something is off, you don't need permission to disengage.

I am of the idea that part of defining what

something is should also include defining what it is not.

Dating does not mean a commitment of any type.
It is not a contractual agreement. It is completely up to you to decide the terms. But make sure you are deciding, or someone will decide for you. Your heart is more valuable than that.

Dating does not require sexual intimacy to be successful.
In fact, intimacy often rushes things, causing us to participate in an emotional bonding process that you have yet to cognitively process. Sex is a glue that is meant to help you deal with an imperfect person. But if this person has not committed to you, and you are glued to them...or worse, they are glued to you, though they know they should not be...nothing good comes of this. You know. You've seen it.

Dating does not mean you're no longer single. Honestly, you are single or you are married. Any other title in regards to relationship growth is either preparing for marriage, or helping you to enjoy being single.

I know this is a tough one to accept, but think about it. If one can decide one morning, after they have been "together" for three years, that he or she prefers to be single, is that a commitment, really? It could be for a legitimate reason. It could be just because the sky is a darker shade of blue that morning. But they can walk away, and you would be scorned if you overreacted. You thought they were your boyfriend/girlfriend, but in reality, you were acting as a husband/wife. You can't help yourself. You have invested all this emotional, physical and sexual energy. And then, one day, the love of your life just shrugs … and walks away. Some will say that can happen in any marriage. I say that it must be a couple that didn't read this book!

Seriously, if a boyfriend/girlfriend is telling you there is no difference, then why haven't they proposed? We all know there is a difference in terms of accountability and intention.

Dating the right way does not mean you will not be disappointed.

You may really like a person and may be very compatible in theory. But when it is time to have the talk that leads from dating to courtship, the person declines. They decide that they would prefer just being friends. This is good, healthy, and safe, but it is sometimes disappointing.

Do not be afraid to say that out loud. This disappointment is very different from heartbreak. You only risked what you could gamble, and both of you walk away unscarred. The temptation will be to try and seduce the person. Stop that. You are better than treating yourself like that. Keep working on you. Another will come.

Dating does not have a time limit.
Take your time, but keep your boundaries. And when things shift . . . have that conversation. Feelings change, and that is okay.

Dating is literally just getting to know a person.
That is it. That is all. Unless you are signing up for a dramatic experience, it should be relatively painless. Dating is fun, exciting, but it must be explored with wisdom, intentionality, and discernment.

Courting is deciding that this person you have dated is someone you can build a future with, and both of you are actively building on this decision.

Marriage is deciding after the interview and audition, that your companies should merge and cover more territory. Remember, our relationships are our most precious resource. Make sure you are taking care of yours.

About the Author

Travis Bryant Jr. lives in Kansas City, MO with his wife and two daughters. He is an interpersonal consultant for TouchKC, LLC, as well as a program manager for a parent aide agency. He has worked with countless families over the last 15 years in his mission to create and rejuvenate interpersonal and intrapersonal health through various platforms and services. Currently, Travis is finishing his masters degree in Marriage and Family Therapy.

FOR MORE INFORMATION ON SERVICES
THAT TOUCHKC PROVIDES,
VISIT **TOUCHKC.COM**.

ALSO, TO READ INTRIGUING ARTICLES
WHERE CONTRIBUTORS DISCUSS INTERPERSONAL
TOPICS AND TEACH HOW TO MAINTAIN YOUR
RELATIONSHIPS WHILE MANAGING YOUR
PERSONAL GROWTH
VISIT **ENTERPERSONAL.COM**.

Quote Citations

- Blaise Pascal Quotes. (n.d.). BrainyQuote.com. Retrieved December 18, 2018, from BrainyQuote.com Web site: https://www.brainyquote.com/quotes/blaise_pascal_138831

- Alvin Toffler Quotes. (n.d.). BrainyQuote.com. Retrieved December 18, 2018, from BrainyQuote.com Web site: https://www.brainyquote.com/quotes/alvin_toffler_107879

- Maria Bamford Quotes. (n.d.). BrainyQuote.com. Retrieved December 18, 2018, from BrainyQuote.com Web site: https://www.brainyquote.com/quotes/maria_bamford_571868

- Benjamin Franklin Quotes. (n.d.). BrainyQuote.com. Retrieved December 18, 2018, from BrainyQuote.com Web site: https://www.brainyquote.com/quotes/benjamin_franklin_138217

- Ricardo Montalban Quotes. (n.d.). BrainyQuote.com. Retrieved December 18, 2018, from BrainyQuote.com Web site: https://www.brainyquote.com/quotes/ricardo_montalban_190532

- Benjamin Franklin Quotes. (n.d.). BrainyQuote.com. Retrieved December 18, 2018, from BrainyQuote.com Web site: https://www.brainyquote.com/quotes/benjamin_franklin_138217

- Ray Kroc Quotes. (n.d.). BrainyQuote.com. Retrieved December 18, 2018, from BrainyQuote.com Web site: https://www.brainyquote.com/quotes/ray_kroc_402579

- Dinesh Paliwal Quotes. (n.d.). BrainyQuote.com. Retrieved December 18, 2018, from BrainyQuote.com Web site: https://www.brainyquote.com/quotes/dinesh_paliwal_908674

- Herta Muller Quotes. (n.d.). BrainyQuote.com. Retrieved December 18, 2018, from BrainyQuote.com Web site: https://www.brainyquote.com/quotes/herta_muller_571074

THANK YOU FOR READING
AND PURCHASING THIS BOOK

TouchKC

We aim to create
valuable services that allow for
interpersonal development.